Getting fit and healthy has never been easier!

Laugh the kilos away with this refreshing new approach to Fitness and Health.

Author and Fitness Instructor *Trixie Bloom* **combines real exercises with plenty of humour to help the medicine go down.**

Printed by CreateSpace, An Amazon.com Company
Published by Farquhar Publishing
Copyright © 2016 Loulou Farquhar. All rights reserved, including the right to reproduce, distribute, or transmit in any form, or by any means. For information regarding subsidiary rights, please contact the Publisher.

Website: farquharpublishing.com
Email: linton@farquharpublishing.com
ISBN 978-0-9935525-3-3

These workouts should not be attempted by the very young, old, or sick. You should consult your doctor prior to commencing any exercise regime.

"Always drink water during any workout. Build up to all the stretches. Go as far as comfortable with all the exercises. Don't push yourself and risk injury. It has taken me a long time to get into some of these positions."

Trixie Bloom

TRIXERCISE

Part One - Loving Yourself Hurts
by
Trixie Bloom

"Life should be viewed in humour-vision."

Trixie Bloom

Contents

1. Before and After
2. Introduction
3. Acknowledgements
4. Items you will need
5. Disclaimer
6. Warnings
7. Aerobics
9. 30 Second Workout
11. Neck Bender
13. Aeroplane
15. The Hangover
17. The Yoni Stretch
18. The Pushback
19. The Big Toe Stretch
20. Back Groin Stretch
21. Tummy Tuck
22. Crouching Trixie
23. The Windbreaker
25. The Eye-Opener
26. Ladies' Yawn
27. Deep Thrusting Lift
28. Praying to be Slim
29. Diets
37. Trixie's Advice and Help
41. Pearls
43. But seriously...

T.T.
Trixie's Tips
These stars indicate handy hints.

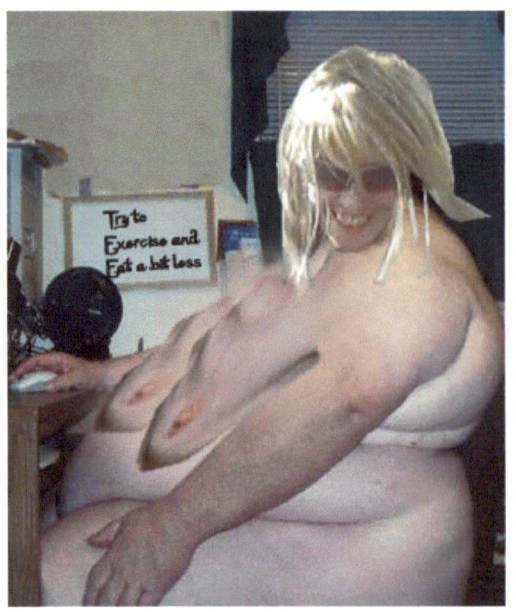 

BEFORE
Yes, that was me.
I know.

AFTER
Just look at me now !

Naturally, we are all different, so please don't expect the same results that I have, amazingly, achieved. You have helped yourself immeasurably today by purchasing a copy of this book.

In just under 7 and a half hours, I was able to achieve these results by listening to my own advice. I did the exercises and followed the diets. I am so glad I listened to myself.

INTRODUCTION

Hi!

I'm Trixie Bloom, world famous author and exercise guru. My background history began when I began to study exercise. For a whole, terrifying 3 years, I *was* that creature in the before photo.

During my 'Whale' period, I studied countless videos and books about exercise. I heard myself telling these disgusting lies;

"I have a bubbly personality."
"I am big-boned"
"My family are fat."
"I am happy like this."

Finally, I managed to go on a gruelling 3 day exercise course. I have never looked back since.

Looking at this new, stunning Me, you *know* it worked.

Acknowledgements

I would like to thank *Myself* for my tireless struggle against the onslaught of Fat.

Before I listened to *Myself*, my existence was a hippo in a hammock. Thanks to *Me*, I am now a leaping gazelle.

Items you will need

❈ A swimming pool
❈ Running Machine
❈ 1 chair (I have used a Chippendale, but any old chair will do)
❈ 1 bottle of Holy Water
❈ Exercise Mat by Soul Flotation. They contour your body with tiny pockets of trapped air that has been imported from a Buddhist retreat in the Himalayas. A snip at only £365.95
❈ Summer house in the mountains
❈ Exercise clothes. I have mine designed by Guy Gizzard of Peacock St. Mayfair.

Disclaimer

I accept no responsibility if this life-changing book does not work for you.

You must wait for my sequel, try harder and stop snivelling.

All the exercises in this book can be performed by someone else.

Warnings

At no point during any time of the day, should these exercises be performed. All exercises are for all ages, 1 - 103 years old. If they do not work for you, it would be a complete failure on your part. I have given you my everything.

Injuries

If you have *ever* hurt yourself, (For example, I once broke an eyelash clean in half, and had to have a month off work.) then make an appointment with your already overburdened doctor.

If you are in a wheelchair, or permanently on crutches, do NOT attempt these exercises.

Pregnant women

I wouldn't bother doing this workout, its already too late for you.

Aerobics

There's no getting out of this. All that jelly wobble needs to be jiggled...

A good healthy swim in your pool for about twenty minutes, 3 times a week, will firm up your slack turkey muscles.

If this is too much for you, simply splash around in the shallow end creating a feeling that you are, at least, doing *something*.

If you haven't got access to a pool, just swim in your local sewage reservoir, and strengthen your immune system into the bargain.

Running is an ideal activity, filling your lungs with good clean air. Simply flick the switch on your running machine, and take a gentle 15 minute jog.

If you don't have a running machine, just jog 3 times around your swimming pool. If you don't have a swimming pool, RUN to and from the sewage reservoir.

If this is all too much for you, simply sit in a chair, and watch *any* machine for 15 minutes, 3 times a week.

30 Second Workout

Squeezing it in when you're short on time...

Starting position. Breathing mindfully, start to raise arms.

Count 5, ending up in this position.

Counting another 5, raise arms above your head.

Sitting back, bend forward from the waist, arms straight out in front for 5 seconds

Slowly come back up, arms above your head again for the count of 5.

Lower arms to the count of 5

Continue down for another 5, and you're done!

This workout does absolutely no good at all, but in your mind, you'll feel healthier and fitter, and that's what matters.
You can also say in good conscience to friends and colleagues, that you *do* work out.

Please remember to breathe throughout this routine.

Neck Bender

This gentle warm-up may be done whilst standing or seated.

Starting position. Back straight and shoulders relaxed.

Slowly turn your head towards your right.

Then, slowly to the left, before returning to centre.

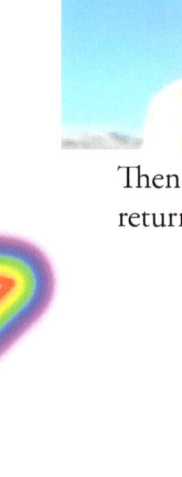

T.T.
Drink plenty of Holy Water. It contains less calories. Simply ask your local monastery or convent.

Repeat 3x

Return your head to the centre, and repeat on your left.

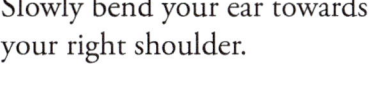

Slowly bend your ear towards your right shoulder.

Slowly tilt your head forward , and return to centre again.

T.T.

Always nibble.
Never chew.

The Aeroplane

This is for your waist.

Repeat 3x

Starting position.

Lift arms into a Y shape.

Bend your waist and tilt to your right.

End position.

Repeat to your left.

Return to the Y-shape.

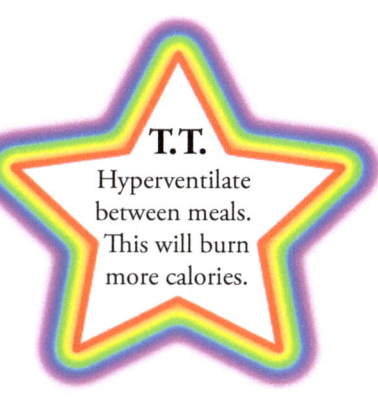

T.T.
Hyperventilate between meals. This will burn more calories.

The Hangover

Let the weight of your alcoholically poisoned body and head guide you down, and gravity will do the rest.

When down, hold for a count of 4.

Starting position. Feet roughly in line with your shoulders.

Raise arms above your head.

Let your head guide you down.

Lower your arms back to the sides.

Keep your knees nice and relaxed as you return to this position.

Let yourself hang heavily.

T.T.
Do not show ANY facial expressions, as they will create wrinkles.

Yoni Stretch

This full, deep action engages and warms up even your Sub-Yoni areas. Move slowly and smoothly.

Repeat 4x

Starting position. This can be performed with a chair, or free-standing.

Slowly lower yourself, keeping your back nice and straight.

Knees over your ankles. Don't go down lower than this, and rise up slowly.

T.T.
Surround yourself with fat people.

The Pushback

This engages all your action muscles, pumping them plump.

Starting position, with the aid of a chair.

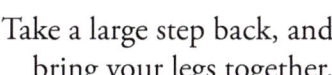

Take a large step back, and bring your legs together.

Allow the knees to bend a little, as you try to push your arms and back fully straight. Hold for 4 breaths. Then step forward into the start position.

T.T.
Worry and stress are guaranteed to shed the weight, so don't stop worrying, no matter what anyone says.

Big Toe Stretch

This is a ballet exercise which strengthens and stretches your feet.

Repeat 4x

Starting position.

Take your right foot to the side, and up onto your big toe tip.

Bring right foot back to centre, and repeat with the left.

T.T.
Only go out after dark to avoid the embarrassment of being seen.

Back Groin Stretch

Stretch your vertebrae, pelvis and legs with this spinal twist.

Repeat 2-4x

Starting position.

Cross your right leg over your left thigh. Hold your crossed leg with your left hand.

Twist your waist to the right, and place your right hand on the floor. Hold for a count of 5 and return to the starting position. Repeat on the opposite side.

T.T.
Think Thin.

Tummy Tuck

The gentle pulling action helps to lift your abdominals.

Repeat 3x

Starting position.

Holding the backs of your thighs, round your back, pulling your stomach towards your spine.

Slowly return to start position.

T.T.
Fruit must be organically grown, but make sure no human has touched it.

Crouching Trixie

The gentle pulsing action activates your abdominals

Starting position.

Arms out in front and twist your waist to your left.

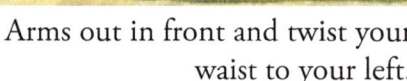

Place hands on the floor, and lower yourself down as illustrated. Hold for a count of 3, and return to the start position. Repeat on the opposite side.

T.T.
Between meals, occupy your mind with thoughts of all the foods you cannot have.

The Windbreaker

These simple knee lifts work your hips and purge trapped wind.

Repeat 3-6x

Starting position.

Slowly bring your right knee towards your chest.

Back to the start position, and repeat with the other leg.

Slowly return to the start/end position.

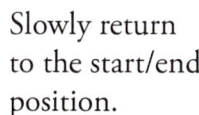

No further than illustrated.

Now lift both legs together and bring towards your chest.

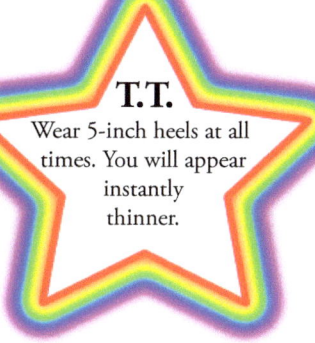

T.T.
Wear 5-inch heels at all times. You will appear instantly thinner.

Eye Opener

This will tighten virtually everything below the waist.

Repeat 4-6x

Starting position. Legs up, toes pointed skyward.

Keeping toes pointed, slowly open as wide as you can.

Flex the feet and slowly close legs together, back to the start position.

T.T.
For the true taste of vegetables, just ask your pilot to fly you to the country of origin.

Ladies' Yawn

This strengthens your most important regions.

Repeat 3-6x

Starting position.

Place your hands on your knees and pull them apart slowly.

Knees in line with hips, hold for a count of three before returning to the starting position.

T.T.
The larger your breasts, the smaller everything else looks. Invest in a very large bra, and pad it out.

Deep Thrusting Lift

This strengthens stomach, buttocks and pelvis.

Repeat 3-5x

Starting position. Legs hip-distance apart.

Tighten your stomach, and lift your hips slowly off the floor.

Lift as high as possible and hold for a count of 3. Lower slowly back to the starting position.

T.T.
Conceal your size by wearing a tent.

Praying to be Slim

This one is for strengthening your mind *and* body.

Repeat 2x

Starting position.

Begin to sit back, taking your buttocks towards your feet, your arms stretched out in front.

Stay in this position for a count of 10. Long enough for your prayer to be heard.

T.T.
Apply a nicotine patch, they are brilliant for suppressing your appetite.

Diets.

These are some of the top diets I have tried, before stumbling upon my own, brilliant health plan. Be warned, some of these diets will have you living in the ladies room.

1. Vegetable juice

Choose lots of yummy vegetables. Don't actually *eat* these items, just boil the soul out of them, then throw them away, keeping the liquid. Store it in the fridge until the smell resembles a blocked drain. Then begin to drink this foul liquid 3 times a day.
Do this as long as you can stand it.

2. Egg and Grapefruit

Eat only egg and grapefruit for 1 whole week. I think you can imagine the consequences of this one. (A good supply of toilet tissue is required.)

3. Meat Only

Recommended for up to 6 months. (Time to follow, not age.) Only Meat, nothing else. After 3 months I felt like an entire farmyard had moved into my colon, whereupon I ended it abruptly.

4. Fruit Only

This has double benefits. You will tone your legs running to the bathroom, and strengthen your stomach with the tensing.

5. Sachet Diets

Any diet that comes in a sachet and needs to be mixed and drunk, is beyond repulsive. This wannabe milkshake or soup is meant to provide the same nutritional value as 3 meals a day. That non-tasting, insubstancial, lumpy thin liquid that sticks to your throat as you swallow just reminds me of too many horrid things.

6. Cabbage Diet

The cabbage, green or red, can be cooked in many different ways. Saving and drinking the stewed cold cabbage juice will guarantee weight loss. This fart-smelling liquid/food will have you vomiting into submission. Follow this one as long as you can stand it.

7. No Dairy

Basically anything that comes out of an animal is forbidden, but not the unfortunate creature itself. Follow this for 2 weeks.

8. Gastric Band

This is one of my personal favourites. Simply risk your life by being put under anaesthetic, have an elastic band popped round your guts, and Voilà! Watch the weight slide off.

9. Trixercise Health Plan

The most effective diet I have ever tried. If you follow this, in conjunction with my exercises and health tips, you cannot fail. No need to chop off a limb, or never leave the house. I am here to help you. Throw away every useless fad diet/exercise book you ever bought, and follow this instead. It's the only one you will ever need again. (Apart from all my sequels.)

Simply take my word for it, look at me, I'm 65, living proof it works.

Dangerous Desserts

All these beautifully presented desserts were prepared by my sexy Chef -
Henri Jacques Phillipe Petit Voilá!

These are highly dangerous if you are on a diet, and even looking at these pictures can increase your weight. If you are on a diet, look away NOW.

If you have attained perfection like me, then by all means indulge your eyes.

Chocolate Dribble Desire
Calories: **15000** per muffin
Fat Content: **5** bucket's worth

Orgasmic Ice
Calories: **1000** per teaspoon
Fat Content: **5** bucket's worth

Creamy Goo
Calories: **1.5 Million** per 1oz serving
Fat Content: **Pure Fat** - Massive overload

Sweet Purple Joy
Calories: Off the chart.
Fat Content: Ditto

Sexy Bloom Cupcake
Calories: Only **5** per cake
Fat Content: 0.5g per cake
(Personally made for me, low in everything, I can eat as many as I want.)

Squirming Carrot Pleasure
Calories: Only **9000** per muffin
Fat Content: Roughly **Half** a Cow.

Daily Recipes

All these recipes are called *Nouvelle Cuisine*. It's what posh people like me eat. So don't think of these dishes as part of a diet, but console yourself that in some way you can be the same as upper class people. Just like my exercises I have dumbed down my recipes, desperately trying to keep them cost-effective, which was extremely challenging.

Starters

1 extra large glass (450 ml) of **Red Wine** (Any peasant vintage)

or

Nettle Soup. Place a sprig of nettles in a bowl and pour boiling water over them.

or

1 soldier of **Toast** with ½ a pipette of tasteless margarine spread on it.

Main Courses

Un Poisson avec Féves au Lard

Serves - 1 adult and 1 child
Preparation time - 4 hours

Ingredients
1 sardine, boned
3 baked beans
¼ teaspoon of sauce reserved from the beans.

Splay open the sardine and arrange the beans on top.
Drizzle the bean sauce over the dish, and serve immediately.

Pomme de Terre Friteuse avec La Tomate Tranche

Serves - 16 people
Preparation time - 6 ½ minutes

Ingredients
1 potato
1 tomato

Peel the potato, and cut 3 medium sized chips from it. Fry in deep oil until golden. Lay a thin slice of tomato down flat and arrange the chips so that they orbit it.

Oeuf du Sauce Rouge

Serves - 3, possibly with enough left for a small dog such as a terrier.

Preparation time - Try to start at least 24 hrs in advance.

Ingredients
1 egg
1 bottle or sachet of tomato sauce

Boil the egg for at least an hour. Keep topping up the water if you have to. After it has cooled, peel and cut in half. Throw one half away, and drizzle tomato sauce over the one you keep.

Sweets and Puddings

Place a teaspoon of yogurt artfully on a serving dish, and mount the raisin upon the top.

Yaort du Raisin

Serves - 1
Preparation time - 9 ¼ minutes

Ingredients
Any low-fat yogurt
1 raisin

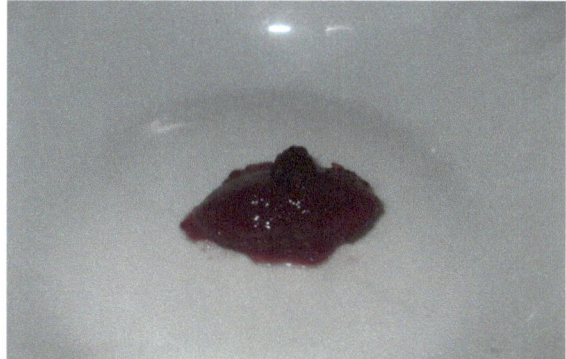

The same as for **Yaort du Raisin.**

Confiture du Raisin Fraise

Serves - 2 adults, 1 baby
Preparation time - 7 minutes, plus a 1 min. interval

Ingredients
Jam, strawberry only.
1 raisin

Slice the apple roughly as thin as a lemon slice. Shave a tiny shard of chocolate off and garnish the apple to taste.

Pomme du Chocolat

Serves - 8
Preparation time - 13 ¼ minutes

Ingredients
An Apple
Dark Chocolate

Trixie's Advice and Help

Being the global role model that I am, many people find comfort in my pearls of wisdom.

"Nobody loves you when you're fat. And stop snivelling."

Trixie Bloom.

When I was fat, I was viewed as one of life's stains. Now I am thin, I have achieved nothing. Until now.
Let me shoot you some of my pearls.

Dining Out

This can be very tempting if you are on a diet. Just refuse any food whilst watching your friends enjoy theirs. Sniff in all the lovely aromas. Smell is calorie free, after all.

Chocolate

Follow these easy rules, and enjoy yourself.

a) 2 chunks of dark, black chocolate between 10am and Midday hold no fear and can be happily enjoyed.

b) 1 ½ chunks between Midday and 4pm, should be nibbled with caution and an underlying anxiety.

c) Even 1 chunk between 4pm and bedtime is sure to bring horror and dread, and is guaranteed to add weight while you sleep.

Take the scales from your eyes

Never, ever own a set of bathroom scales, or even get on any, if you feel you are overweight, because this will make you even more miserable than you already are.

If you are a perfect weight, on the other hand, then you should definitely invest in some scales, and weigh yourself every day to make sure you maintain your weight.

If you are travelling away, take your scales with you. You simply cannot chance anyone else's. Always weigh yourself naked, after the first two visits to the ladies room. This still applies when you are travelling away from home.

Here is a handy chart you can refer to to find your perfect weight.

Height	Ideal Weight
Small (under 4ft/122cm)	16 kg/35 lb
Medium (4-6ft/122-183cm)	21.5 kg/47 lb
Big (above 6ft/183cm)	29 kg/64 lb

In Greedy Ants

Always scrutinize the ingredients on your food to make sure they contain **No** gluten, **No** lactose, **No** saturated fat, **No** sugar, and that they are **Low**-fat, **Low**-calorie and **Only** contain friendly bacteria, and you can't go wrong. Don't forget to ask your Personal Trainer to set a healthy menu for your Chef to work with.

Surgery

My view is that people who are born ugly have generally adapted well, mostly staying indoors, living in remote areas etc. If you have no such excuse, and you are lazy, and don't wish to attempt to rectify your bodily indiscretions, then by all means go for the 'Under the knife' approach. I feel the same about liposuction. However I do have empathy for those who have lost a lot of weight and have to tuck their stomach into their socks. Then I would say go for surgery.

Tape Measure

If the tape measure doesn't reach together when you put it round your waist, it's time to start shopping for that tent.

Pearls

🎀 Some people say dieting is a dirty word. Chunky people will always say this, and any advice from them should be completely ignored.

🎀 Sugar (Any colour) is a filthy, dirty substance, and one of the most dangerous and addictive substances on the planet. Stay well away.

🎀 Pray nightly - 'If you can't make me slim, not even with Trixie's help, to make everyone else fat instead.'

🎀 Even if you are severely ill, a spray-on tan works wonders.

🎀 Remember, if you cant laugh at yourself, how can you expect others to stop?

Lastly, I cannot stress enough, that

Life is for Living! (Only if you're thin.)

Trixie Bloom on her '97 PAIN Tour of Australia, whipping down under into a frenzy.

But seriously...

I have battled hard against my weight my entire life. I have always loved sweet things, and became very down on myself in my teenage years. In the end, I chose to become a professional fitness instructor, and began to study healthy eating.

I have personally tried all the diets in this book, (Apart from the Drastic Gastric Band) and I have used my English sense of irony to humorize some of the ludicrous advice I have been given.

The best advice I could offer, is to be realistic with yourself regarding your natural body shape, height and genetics. For example, I am comfortable with my one breast that is bigger than the other. It doesn't mean I'm ready to join the Freak Circus. I also accept that when I lose weight, it always rapidly disappears from my face, giving me a haunted appearance, whilst my child bearing hips prevail. There is not much I can do about my genetics, and natural ageing. It is hard to change our habits overnight. I say the same about food; Be honest about what you can achieve. Do not deprive yourself of a little bit of what you enjoy.

The exercises I have chosen to put in this book are simple, and should be risk-free. I highly recommend doing the exercises in front of a mirror, as it helps to get the position, or form, as perfect as possible. They will help you to start an easy, achievable exercise plan. Again, be realistic. Even if it's only once every fortnight, at least you have begun.

I am with you every step of the way.

Good luck!

Trixie Bloom ♥

If you enjoyed this book, please leave a favourable review on Amazon.

About the author

Trixie Bloom is a Fitness instructor and Dance teacher turned Author/Comedienne. Once a socialite, she now lives as a hermit in the wilds of Andalusia, and spends her spare time working with disadvantaged children in remote pueblos.

Other titles by *Trixie Bloom*

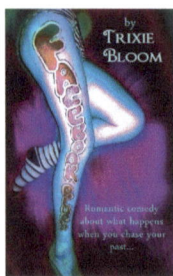

Facebook Blues is a romantic comedy about what happens when you chase your past.

Accident prone misfit *Lauren*, is dizzy and sexually intoxicating, although she believes herself incapable of love. Deeply bored and unimpressed with her life, she delves into her past, looking for her first love, *David*.

More than twenty years since they last met, she is about to re-enter his world, uninvited, with life changing consequences for everyone around her...

This book has an accompanying playlist, and an original song 'embedded' within. At the appropriate moment in the story, either scanning a QR code or clicking the link (Paperback or Kindle.) will enable the reader to listen along with the characters.

Connect with me

Author Blog - **trixiebloom.com**
Twitter Handle - **@trixie_bloom**
Facebook Page - **facebook.com/trixiebloom**
Amazon Author Profile - **amazon.com/author/trixiebloom**
Goodreads Profile - **goodreads.com/author/show/15165037.Trixie_Bloom**

www.ingramcontent.com/pod-product-compliance
Lightning Source LLC
Chambersburg PA
CBHW041757040426
42446CB00005B/239